9/9

*Rowanne,
My fourth book —
And the first one with
some of my journal
entries. ♡ Robert*

Sky of Dreams

Robert A. Cozzi

SKY OF DREAMS Copyright © 2017 by Robert A. Cozzi.
All rights reserved.

Printed in the United States of America.

No part of this book may be used or reproduced in any manner whatsoever without written permission except in the case of brief quotations embodied in critical articles or reviews.

For information, address Beach Umbrella Publishing 1834 SE 5th Street, Cape Coral, Florida 33990

LIBRARY OF CONGRESS CATALOGING IN PUBLICATION DATA

Cozzi, Robert A.

    Sky of Dreams /by Robert A. Cozzi

ISBN- 13:978-0692961810

ISBN- 10:069296181X

First Edition: October 2017

FOREWORD

A Chorus of Optimism

By Loretta Obstfeld, Poet

The opening lines of "On the Heels of the Morning Light," in this remarkably optimistic and heartfelt collection by Robert A. Cozzi, read:

> Things are changing
>
> New sounds fill the air
>
> And the world around me
>
> Is coming alive again

In the poem, the sounds are of nature stirring. But to me, this observation is the essence of art and its effect on the world. We learned long ago that direct statements and pontifications often lack the power to incite insight and affect change, whether in the individual or in society. The parent warns the child not to be cruel to an outcast schoolmate and is ignored. But that child sees the cruel behavior in *Me, Earl, and the Dying Girl,* and is suddenly kinder. It is the finely honed art that offers a fresh perspective to let us see who we really are and what we need to do.

The human compulsion to manifest thought and emotion in some physical form—from cave drawings to the Sistine Chapel, from whistling to Gregorian chants—is how we celebrate what is good in life and calibrate what needs to change. When Cozzi says, "New sounds fill the air," he could just as easily be referring to the voices of all the artists—himself included—that form a chorus to inspire us to see the world more clearly, to embrace the vagaries of life more boldly, and to face the treacheries of humanity more kindly.

If art has the power to change us in general, Cozzi's art specifically nudges us to see value in relationships—lovers, friends, and family. And even when his poems touch our hearts with sadness, there is a fundamental celebration of humanness that is inspiring and refreshing.

It is this soaring chorus of optimism tempered with realism that makes us proclaim, "And the world around me/Is coming alive again." These poems are a singular voice in that chorus that makes the world come alive to the reader in a way that they will cherish and never forget.

Dedication:

I would like to dedicate this book of work:

To my forever friends, Kirat Randhawa and Danielle Hafler Porosky for their unconditional love and constant support.

To my Mom and Dad, I miss you every day.

To Annmarie, Michael, Nicholas, and Nick with love.

Acknowlegements:

I would like to express my thanks to:

Gerard Yatcilla, Mary Healy Davis, Ian Tompkins, Trish Bizink Abell, Donna Catanzaro, Michelle Osterberg, Lisa Hafler, Larry Osterberg, Jo Ann Carra, Jim Kurzawa, Jerome Gonzalez, Bryan Glenn, Jamie Treglown, Pete Donatelli, Amparo Mendoza, Jeanne Emerick, Chris Loder, Patti Hearon Esler, Ely Jaffe, Rob Syvret, Sean Williams, Matthew Ryan Woolfrey, Anne Laird, Paul Kocum, Tai Babilonia, Loretta Obstfeld, Ed Burgos, Annemarie Biondi, Meg Lee, Christine Kelly, Karen Clarkson, Glenn Randall, Austin Hein, Christopher Wolfson, Jaime Schneider, Mary King Treglown, Mike Bennett,

Bonnie Caryn Ensor, Pam Evans, Teresa Boyd, LaShawn Scott, Kenya Francios, Phillip Wilcher, Jack Babineau, Jane Merkwaz Babineau, Anthony Keating, Sandy Iammatteo, Walt Clarkson, Rob Shipley, A.S.Angelo, Kristin Nascelli, Suzzie Magdaline Paramito, Stevie Nicks, The Town Book Store, my Saturday morning story hour kids from the library, and my Facebook and Instagram followers and friends.

AUTHOR'S NOTE

After a somewhat tumultuous year, I finally feel like writing again. I am starting here and I am not sure what will come out or where I will finish.

Would you want to know where or how or when you finish? It is a moot point of course. Maybe we all know but it gets forgotten so that we can live our lives. I believe that there are so many things outside of our realm of understanding. We are trapped here in these soul keepers. These bodies and minds and chemistry are limited. I believe we are allowed glimpses into other realms but mostly we ignore these feelings and intuitions.

There is more. I don't know how I know or if this is just wishful thinking but there is more. I just know.

You can fall into the knowing or you can spend your life resisting the obvious.

I really do feel that everyone has a purpose ...a reason for being ...a path. I have been fighting mine for as long as I can remember. I am not sure why. Maybe I think I am unworthy.

I remember the first time I took a walk along the puddle-ridden path in the woods behind our house. It was right after we moved to Westfield. I was 8 years old and I wanted to see where it ended. There was that irresistible curiosity to see the conclusion. And then... standing at the end of it...I saw the same things I had seen as I walked along the middle part. I saw the exact same reflection staring back at me.

Isn't it funny....we search and search for....where the path goes and then... in the end...we stand and face the same reflection we had been seeing all along. We have traveled but we are somehow the same.

I am not anyone special and yet I feel this so strongly. It is hard for me to explain. It is just a knowing. It is looking at my life and knowing all this stuff...all this sometimes horrible...seemingly unexplainable stuff has a purpose...has meaning. It is quite an epiphany. Things happen and you get caught up in the messy details of a life which does not slow down just so you can catch up. It keeps going and pulling you with it, but in the meantime, this path is still waiting.

I guess all this would make more sense with the holes filled in....so....if I could share my life....write it all down...in doing so.... I would walk my path.

Sometimes I do feel so grateful that I have made it this far, so there must be a reason.

I hope you enjoy reading my words. Thank you for purchasing SKY OF DREAMS.

Robert A. Cozzi

NEW HOPE

The warm sun

Rises over the vast horizon

Bringing hope to all fears

Looking up at the denim blue sky

With new hope

His faith reappears

STRENGTH BENEATH MY FEET

For Jamie

Like a high wire artist

I am balanced

Amid the turmoil

The thundering sky

The biting winds

The street and its abashment

I find peace where I stand

Feeling the strength beneath my feet

FALLING

I am inspired by constellations

Fallen

As diamonds cast

Reflecting galaxies gravitating around a luminous moon

The light of your eyes is mesmerizing

Making me fall

As a drunken fool

In love with you

THE GAZE

Looking over my shoulder

That faraway gaze

Breaks me

Every edge digs sharply

Deepens as I breathe

Haunts me as I close my eyes

Without words

You say goodbye

Before I have the chance

To say hello

IRREPARABLE

My heart is a worn out blanket

Irreparable

But perfect for someone

Who doesn't mind the holes

BEFORE THE DUST CAN SETTLE ONTO HIS HEART

It is not the sense of loneliness

But the twinge of desire awakening him

Before the sun drifts in

To his pitch-black room

How many mornings

Has he felt the sun filling the window shades

With magnificent light he could not feel

Because he had nobody next to him to share its brilliance

But before the dust can settle onto his heart

He remembers something his mother once told him,

"Love arrives exactly when love is supposed to"

And that brings his smile back …

BLUE WHITE FIRE

Each embrace

Warms my skin

With assurances

Of uninhibited desire

Wet, steamy kisses

Drench my lover's body

And burn as hot

As blue white fire

TRELLISED HEART

A trellised heart

Offers only walls of goodbye

To the other heart

Standing underneath

The evening's entrenched stars

EMPTY SPACES

We are naturally drawn to that which is hidden

We see a canvas filled with colors but in the corner there is a small, clean, unpainted space. Our eyes go there first.

Our ears hear that pause of silence in the midst of the discord of buzzing conversation. We listen.

We feel the air brush by from the hand that almost touches us … and we yearn for that connection.

We hold that moment right before a kiss … that unbearable torment of waiting … before ending all fantasy.

We are instinctually driven to seek out the pauses … the empty spaces … for the simple reason that … they fill us …

SUN SPECKLED SATURDAY

Just listen to the quiet roar

On this sun speckled Saturday

Wide open books lounge in the lonely corners

Of this library

You can hear the clash of cymbals

Crashing in the distance

While fleeting armies of thoughts

March in between bound pages of words

This is that moment in time

On the cusp of adventure

When you know you see so much more

In the clouds of sunlight

A DIFFERENT KIND OF LOVE

The first day that I knew you

I was filled

With every anxiety

Every intoxicating pleasure

Every regret of self-control

I was haunted

Afraid

Ashamed

But it was the beginning of a different kind of love

So pure and true and real

You are

The beginning and the end

How wonderful

That you are

So much more

Than the first day I knew you

BOOKSTORE CORNER

On this Saturday afternoon

At the Barnes and Noble

A young man sitting in the corner catches my eye

The slow recession of light from the window blind

Makes his sadness illuminate

I take out my writing tablet

And I begin to pen his story

With his head bent low

He sits there alone

Seeking love

In the pages of the book

That he holds tightly in his hands

Happiness

Is unknown to him

Still, he keeps reading

Inside his solitude

He hopes to find the key

To what his life is missing

And

Just when I think I have it all figured out

An attractive young woman enters the bookstore

Making a beeline for the young man

His face lights up as their eyes meet

I watch as she brushes the hair away from his forehead

And kisses him gently

Love consumes the room

I look at the floor and smile

Elated that I had been so wrong

BACK TO EACH OTHER'S EMBRACE

The moon shines so brightly in your brown eyes

Making the night sky rise softly

I can almost see forever

When you look at me this way

The stars look just like jewels above you

Adorning your beautifully chiseled face

Tonight the moonbeams guide the way

Back to each other's embrace

LIKE A CHILD'S FIRST WORD

Memories of your laughter

Fill my room tonight

And like a child's first word

It's beautiful

And mesmerizing

SOMETIMES

Sometimes

All of this life

Comes down

To a thin layer

Of twilight snow

Thawing upon

A single twig

THEY FLY!

I sweep away the ashes

The wind captures them

And they swirl

In the moonlight

No longer imprisoned

They fly!

"WHEN THE RAIN WASHES YOU CLEAN YOU'LL KNOW ..."

Outside the streets are slick

The rain has washed away yesterday

Cars fly through puddles

Windshield wipers erase the spatter

He sits in his house alone

Listening to Fleetwood Mac's "Dreams"

Praying for a leaky roof

DROWNING

Road open

Windows down

Speed fast

Drifting images

You in summer rain

Hair falling in your eyes

Wishful thinking

Stale memories

I drown …

GRAND ADVENTURES

It all began with A.A. Milne

And his Winnie the Pooh books

You read them to me every night at bedtime

I wanted to be Christopher Robin so badly!

And I used to daydream of my own adventures

With Pooh, Piglet, Rabbit, and Eeyore

I remember once

When we were driving

I pointed to a small red house

Declaring proudly that it was "Pooh's House"

You smiled and played along

Each and every time we passed that house

My imagination was definitely in full swing back then!

Before I was old enough to go to school

We spent the days together

Often taking the bus into Elizabeth

For those popular sidewalk sales

I remember the bagel store there

And the salt bagel we used to share

That was always warm and right out of the oven

On the way back to the bus stop

We would stop at the Fannie Farmer candy store

Where you would buy for me

Candy cigarettes and fruit slices

A delicious treat for the bumpy bus ride home

I loved our weekly trips

To the library

For the children's story hour

It was there I heard the words of E.B. White for the first time

And fell in love with his books

In winter, we would go ice skating

Sometimes over at the pond

And other times at the big rink

In Warinanco Park

These winter adventures were usually

Followed by cups of hot chocolate with marshmallows

And your homemade Oatmeal Raisin cookies

Later, when I was a teenager

And you were writing your weekly column

In the Suburban News

I was your "editor" and "proof reader"

Duties I was well trained for

Thanks mainly to Mr. Kocum, my 9th grade English teacher

Who, along with you, reawakened my love for books and words

I admired your talent for writing about things that were both relevant and entertaining

I don't think you ever knew what you were going to write about

Until you sat down at the typewriter a few hours before your deadline

And then Dad would drive your finished column down and drop it into the Suburban News mail slot

I began writing because of you

And reading to the kids over at the library

Because of you

The faces of the children I read to today

Remind me of my own face at their age

So wide-eyed and full of wonder

Sitting on the wall

Right above my computer screen

Is a picture of Pooh with Christopher Robin

That reads, "A grand adventure is bound to happen"

It suits us perfectly

Because the times we spent together

Were always grand adventures

CLOSE

You surround me

I am caught up in such a longing

We mesh and flow

We are a symphony

You strum me gently

And there is no turning back

All of my life has been

In preparation for this

You here with me

So close that your sigh

Is but my own breath falling gently

Upon your cheek

CONFESSIONAL PARADE

I wave my hand out the window

And look out at the cloudy sky

I try to tell myself it's only temporary

But in my heart I know it's not

Because it's only the beginning of a confessional parade

WE FALL

We measure our lives in fractions of time. A minute here … a second there … moments lost and days we have not met. Time strings us along as we pull backward towards what we know and what we have been. Impressions give way to unalterable forces of change. We move, at times, against our will and into a future we can never know. We are always reaching for those moments we cannot grasp. Time forces us to release our hold.

And in between moments we fall …

We fall into arms and folds of warmth. We fall into soft eyes and whispers. Our name is called and we strain to hear it for the first time. The chorus echoes through the wind and into the poet's pen. A painter's brush casts the shadows of a lover's lamp lit face. The distance of lips circles around the universe and the world holds its breath for one solitary kiss.

Time comes to reclaim us and march us into space, but for that moment we think ... we know ... we live forever.

DUSK

A burnt auburn dusk yawns

And the ocean breeze dives through us

As we make our way

Down to our spot at the end of the beach

I watch as the incoming surf creates tide pools

In barefooted traces

Your fingers tenderly find my hand

Trapping it in a crossed embrace

An unabashed moon pokes its crescent smiles

Across a fading orange sky

Your blue green eyes sparkle

When I mouth a silent," I love you"

Your reply comes as a head on my chest

And a prolonged sigh

Gingerly, I touch your lips

Nipping them in gentle cadence

Blanketed in the sand

We sit closely together in silence

As the sea composes

The melody of the newborn evening

ON THE HEELS OF THE MORNING LIGHT

Things are changing

New sounds fill the air

And the world around me

Is coming alive again

The frogs are croaking enthusiastically outside my window

Their song is a comforting sound this evening

By dawn, the air is warm again

The chill of yesterday is gone

And the sun sits a little higher up in the Carolina sky today

Returning hope

On the heels

Of the morning light

FALLING AWAY WITH YOU

Inspired by Ed and Gabby

I love your hands

And the way our fingers intertwine

Casting shadows in the room

I love your face

When you smile

And how fast my heart beats

I love the way your arms circle my waist

Running through

Pulling me in close

I love the silence

When no words are needed

And the world around us just falls away

THAT SMILE

The smile comes slowly

But it comes

And I am so glad

That smile

The one where your cheekbones rise and kiss those eyes

The one that makes me feel strange

Holds more depth

Than the words on my page

You tilt your head

Blinking slowly

Until I finally muster up the courage

To meet your stare

THE SUMMER BETWEEN SIXTH AND SEVENTH GRADE

I do remember the summer between sixth and seventh grade. I was nearly twelve years old, still a kid, but nearing adolescence. It was the time of playing outside until the street lights came on. We played endless games of kickball, street hockey on roller skates, capture the flag, kick the can, and freeze tag. If you did manage to stay out past dark, oh what a sense of freedom! Plus you could experience the cool night air punctuated by the blinking lights of fireflies. We would often sit on the porch with a pitcher of cherry Kool-Aid and a bag of chips and talk about everything and nothing at all. We often had sleepovers in the attic with the radio sounds of the Yankee game trailing off into the distance of consciousness. A summer sleep followed, and the moon's pale light would seep through and illuminate your dreams.

My best friend that summer was Chuck, and we spent nearly every waking moment together. Freeze tag was a game that we played with the girls we liked. Jeanne was one of these girls, and Chuck had an awful crush on her. Around Jeanne he was forever tongue-tied and I'd go over and rescue him by killing the awkward silence between them. Back then the girls felt comfortable around me, as did the boys, casting me in the role of messenger between

these two groups. I knew every crush and just about every secret that summer. Chuck and I took plenty of bike rides past Jeanne's house, which was brick with pillars all around with impeccable shrubbery, and a mysterious gold front door. We used to imagine what was behind that door, convinced of its mystical splendor. We rode our ten speed bicycles everywhere that summer. Mine was a red Ross bike with red and white tape on the handlebars and Chuck had a blue Schwinn with red and white tape on the handlebars. We felt like superheroes on those, as if we could conquer anything that crossed our path.

Chuck and I shared a passion for music and Fleetwood Mac, the Eagles, and Elton John were our favorites. We would make the trek down to Music Staff every Tuesday with our paperboy money to see what new albums had been released. We stayed up late to watch The Midnight Special and together we experienced the magic of hearing Stevie Nicks sing "Rhiannon" on live TV. I went to my first rock concert with Chuck and his mom to see Elton John play at Madison Square Garden in August of that summer. We stayed on the most wondrous high well after that show had ended, speaking about the many unforgettable moments to anyone who would listen. Neither of us wanted the summer to end or for Labor Day to arrive, no matter how inevitable that was.

The fireflies caught the night before lie dormant on the bottom of the Hellman's mayonnaise jar with the

punctured lid. September was upon us and our beginning days of junior high school loomed ahead.

For reasons I still find difficult to understand, Chuck and I did not stay friends for much longer after school started that fall. We wandered off in completely different directions. There was never a fight or a falling out. Our friendship just disappeared. Maybe that is the life of a twelve year old. I suppose we both kind of reinvented ourselves that year, leaving our elementary school days far behind.

Even today, as I write these final words, those summer days and nights whisper from a distance, never to be repeated again.

CROSSED PATHS

Time has chosen now

For our paths to cross

To feel the stir and pull

That draws us together

Basking in the glow

Of all that we are

Reaching deep inside

Fulfilling the hunger

That drives us

To tear down the walls

And love with all of our might …

IN LOVE

I lie under your arm, gazing into your deep set green eyes. Your lips move into a slight smile, intoxicated with your sleepy demeanor. Your warm fingers lightly graze my eyebrows, making a pleasurable sensation throughout my body. I let out a sudden yawn and snuggle tighter into your arms. Your body, always warm, makes for a comfortable temperature against mine. I tousle your dark brown hair, and run each finger past strand after strand. You close your eyes softly, but I know you still see me. Your lips look so gentle and they beg for a taste. Soon we are lost in the cool, quiet moment that is our nighttime.

Normally, I cannot relax enough to sleep, but when I am with you, I can. You erase my mind and cast a spell in the most intangible way. My eyes are connected to yours, until they are conquered by my heavy eyelids.

I hold you close to me, protecting you as much as I can, and you do the same for me, as we both drift off to dreamland.

I HAD TO DROWN TO KNOW I WAS ALIVE

I remember

That first dance

Down to every detail

From the song

That was playing

To the way the colored lights

Hung across the ceiling

And lit up your face

The second dance

Scared and mesmerized me

Until I fell beneath your tide

I could not fight

Those waves

I had to drown

To know I was alive

TOO MUCH REALITY

In a candlelit room

Full of books

Talking takes

Way too much

Reality

OLDER

Dipping with each curve

Absorbing the lightness

Inviting folds

Accepting the scars

Earning wrinkles

Ensnaring my mind

Capturing the soul

Melting time

Practicing magic

Whispering myself

Closing my eyes

Touching the peaceful starkness

Memorizing

One

More

Moment

NOTHING

Inside I break

When you look at me

No words fall from your lips

Nothing

Your blank eyes stare in my direction

And I have never felt so alone

CHARLESTON MORNING

We still talk on the phone every few weeks. Some around us remark about how odd that is. That two, who used to be in a love relationship, can be such close friends. But this is absolutely the case.

Hanging up the phone tonight, something you said reminded me of a time many years ago when we both lived in Charleston and were next door neighbors. We had just begun dating a few months before, but we had known one another for more than two years and had been friends first before we became an official couple.

You knocked on my door one morning, waking me before dawn. I open my sleepy eyes and grumble as I make my way to the door. You urge me to hurry up and I grumble some more, wondering why you could not just come back later and let me sleep. Reluctantly, I pull on sweatpants and a hoodie. My eyes are still half closed and I am secretly hoping all of this is just a bad dream.

Out the door we stumble; you in childish wonder, and me in a bit of a huff. The ocean breeze meets us as I follow you through the sand until we come upon two beach chairs. You smile and say, "Sit down." Speechless, I do as instructed. I sit down and you sit beside me. Looking over at me, I notice that childish grin is still on your face. I throw on the hood from my sweatshirt and you pour me hot chocolate from a thermos. I am thinking that you have lost your mind, sitting on the beach in the dark, drinking hot chocolate. Then you say, "Look!" I follow your pointing finger to a spot in the horizon and I get chills … the good kind! Seeing the sun in all of its brilliance, make a slow appearance, rising out of the ocean in orange, yellow, and red perfection, Illuminating the sky, giving life to the darkness. I am speechless in knowing you remembered. You remembered the words I had spoken to you months ago when I told you that I had never seen a sunrise. You remembered!

I didn't say a word. I just sat there watching the day come alive. And with my head resting on your shoulder I knew that something had also come alive in us …

VULNERABLE PASSION

Every little thing about you

Makes me melt

Your soft, dark eyes

The birth mark on the top of your hand

The way you laugh

Or look at me right before being bold

And moving in my direction

My body reacts to your touch

Until all self-control is completely gone

And I am vulnerable

Totally vulnerable

To whatever you decide to do to me next …

ALONE

The stillness of the night

Waked my eyes to loneliness

From where did it come?

This cold moment of emptiness

Leaves me breathless ... searching

Looking for you

Only your scent remains on my heart

It pierces the night

I try to shift my mind elsewhere, but these thoughts still flow

As loneliness lulls me back to sleep

A SOLDIER'S GOODBYE

The tall, blonde, blue-eyed soldier blew on his hands to warm them. Standing at the rail of the troop ship, he watched the others from his unit as they eagerly searched the crowd for loved faces. It would be a long time before they saw those faces again and for some of them it would be forever. He looked out at the morning light glowing on the steam that rose from the warm, crowded bodies below. He knew his parents were not down there. He had recently revealed something serious to them that they did not take too well. All of this left him currently estranged from his family and strained his relationship with his significant other. Leaving the country now was difficult with so many unknowns. He secretly hoped that time would heal all of this pain and perhaps things will be different when he returns home from this tour. So today, he has no special someone to wave goodbye to him, no "girl back home" to write him long letters drenched in perfume and send pictures to tuck inside his helmet. He saw the face of the soldier next to him light up and watched as the soldier's hands started waving madly. Looking down he saw a shapely blonde woman waving just as madly back. It gave

him a twinge, for a moment, and then he spotted his sister, jumping up and down waving an American flag. She had brought two of her friends and they held up the ends of a banner, lettered with his name, "Stephen." To their left, he spotted David whose eyes gleamed with unshed tears. Huge horns sounded and the ship began to move, slowly pulling away from the pier. As people waved and cheered, a band fought to be heard. Stephen locked eyes with his man, who was moving up to join Stephen's sister. Suddenly, the young soldier was waving as wildly as the others. Gazing up at Stephen, David came to attention and brought his arm up to a salute. The young man's eyes misted for a moment, making it hard to focus on the receding figure. Stephen came to attention and returned the salute, holding it until he could no longer see, or be seen by, his loved ones. Their love and pride would be with him where he was going and, if anything could, that would bring him back home.

AS WE BLEED INSIDE

Quiet little steps

One-by-one-by-one

Silence doesn't echo

But it can be so very, very loud

As we bleed inside

<u>EYES LIKE STARS</u>

In my dreams

I see the soft glow of your twinkling eyes

And they are as astounding

As stars that sometimes turn

And fall to the earth

Lighting up the darkness

Until they drift away

Out of sight …

AN UNCONTAINABLE PEACE

If you look inside

You will see the way

My senses perceive the world

Long before our lips met

The taste was a presence I knew

Long before you whispered

My name was in your breath

FOR MARY JOAN GOTTLICK

Your sublime smile

Radiates from the sky

Like the light through a thousand suns

And is worn forever

On the faces of your children

FOREVER

I love the way your eyes explode

When you look at me

And I like the way you bite your bottom lip

When you are nervous

And I like the way your hand fits in mine

More than anything

I like this little world

That happens around us

Whenever we're alone

Sometimes I think

I could live in that world forever

HOW GREAT IS THE HUMAN SPIRIT?

The human spirit is

Only as great

As the hand reaching out to help someone

Or the broadest smile

To dispel sadness

Or

A few extra steps in sync

With a lonely soul

Who has no one to listen

How great is the human spirit?

Each person determines its value

By the reaction shown to others' pain

ONE HEART'S JOURNEY

Tonight

My heart travels

To you

Wiping loneliness

Off your brow ...

<u>THE OTHER SIDE OF THE MIRROR</u>

As darkness walks in

It cloaks the neighborhood in mystery

Putting out the smoldering dregs of day

Across the street

Lights shimmer gently in occupied houses

And a church spire reflects on windy grass

Nights like tonight

Have an edge of fantasy

Waiting to be embraced

Like Alice

I step through the mirror

To another world …

RHIANNON'S WIND

Sun sets

Fingers touch

Heart ponders the idea

Two worlds emerge as one

Differences collide

Acceptance is paramount

Smiling moon calls to the sky

Rhiannon's winds whisper to the rain

Clouds bump into their thoughts

Finally

As darkness falls

A new love is born

WORD DANCE

Words dance in front of my eyes

But I cannot catch them in time

Instead

I watch as they flutter

Circle

And then vanish into the horizon

FATHER'S DAY

Another Father's Day is upon us and I am missing my dad terribly. It is a feeling of simple sadness that possesses me, as opposed to a complex sort of melancholy. I wish I could be like Van Gogh or Plath and turn this despair into something beautiful, but I feel too tired for even that.

My body is a prisoner to this mood....eyes wrung out like an old washrag....my chest is hollowed out and grieving.... legs weak and unsteady.

It breaks my heart that he has missed the last four years of my life ... from all of my new friends that he never got to meet ... to the work I have done at the hotel and the things that I have written and experienced.

There is still beauty in this though. The world slows down. My senses are lulled to visit tiny details...the multi-colored yarn in Dad's hospice afghan...the grain of wood of my desk....the slow recession of light from my window blind...marking the day's end. There are long pauses between my thoughts and words and a sinking into stillness. All is felt and pulled downward.

I am reminded, though, that the pain of sadness isn't as bad as what can follow because a fate worse than sadness is feeling nothing.

At the same time, it's kind of like that old saying about living well being the best revenge against the grief. Finding reasons to wake up happy today and on as many days as I possibly can is my consummate goal. I want to remain curious about the world and experience more and love more because this seems like the most appropriate way to honor a man who was the strongest and sensitive that I have ever known.

BLUEBERRY PANCAKES FIX EVERYTHING

Dragging his feet to the kitchen

He fills the tea kettle

And opens a pack of plain oatmeal

His too large bathrobe

Hangs loosely from his shoulders

Familiar tears fill his eyes

The same ones that come

Most mornings in this second week of April

His whispered words are loud

In the empty kitchen

"God please help me through this day"

The knock on his back door

Only makes him want to crawl back into bed

And under his covers

But he makes his way to the door

To find his friend, Nick

Standing on the porch

Holding a takeout bag from the Sunset Diner

A slight smile begins to form on his face

When his friend hands him the bag and says,

"Blueberry pancakes fix everything!"

DECADENCE

Outside tonight

The sound of rain

Is a form of unsung refuge

Under this blue street light

The innocence between us

Is almost decadent …

BETWEEN LOVE AND DESIRE

Two hearts

Craving to connect

Wanting a harmony

Between love

And desire

Into boardwalk lights and moonbeams

They share a kiss

Under a sky

Made of dreams

OCTOBER BREEZE

Leaning against this old brick wall

I see the mirrored shadows from the two pillars that surround the entrance

As the light from the sun glints on the fallen red and orange leaves

Underneath the chilly October sky

A soft breeze flows

Quietly carrying a sound of happiness on the wind

THE MARVELOUS LAND OF OZ AND THE COOL HIPPIE FAMILY ACROSS THE STREET

Earlier today, I saw a very old edition of, "The Marvelous Land of Oz ", at the library. Seeing it immediately reminded me of a friend I had back when I was 13. Scott was a year younger and lived across the street from me on Normandy Drive. I spent a lot of time over at his house. His family was great. They were hippies dressed as parents, and I loved that! Remember the Mod Squad?
Well…anyway…they had a disheveled house with books everywhere. There were books in every room of that house…very loved and adored books. I remember Scott had all of the Oz books. I was so impressed. I hadn't known that there was more to that story than the famous movie. He and I read the Oz books together, often acting out the adventures we read about.

They had a large attic in their house and for some reason I have always been attracted to attics. I guess because as a little boy we never had a real attic. We lived in houses where the attic had been converted into another bedroom. Anyhow, when Scott would invite me over for sleepovers, we would always sleep

in sleeping bags up in his attic. It was a lot colder up there, even in summer, so we would zip up our sleeping bags and listen to the radio. I don't remember what AM station it was but there was a radio show that told ghost stories and old creepy fairy tales. We would listen and see who would get scared first before eventually falling off to sleep.

On Saturday mornings we would get up and go outside to the woods. Scott's parents didn't believe in television so there were no Saturday morning cartoons to watch. We had to get creative for our entertainment. I suppose it was lucky that neither of us had dull imaginations and we always worked up quite an appetite once lunchtime came around.

Meals were interesting in Scott's house. His parents didn't eat unhealthy things and they did all of their food shopping at a co-op over in Plainfield. His mom, however, made the best peanut butter and banana sandwiches. She knew they were my favorite so we almost always had them for lunch whenever I stayed over.

I remember the day I found out that they were moving away to California after just 3 months in that house, and how upset I was when I heard the news. Over the years, I have often wondered what became of them after they moved. Maybe Scott went on to become a writer, or an actor, or maybe both! I wonder

what he remembers about that summer and our adventures together.

As I sit down and open up the beginning pages of, "The Marvelous Land of Oz", that summer does not seem all that far away anymore.

SKETCH OF US

Your heart beats so quickly

When up against mine

I wonder if our brief embraces

Are enough

To keep you full

The two of us

Are just like a rough sketch

Unfinished and flawed

Simple and beautiful

But so intricately

Woven

Together

STOLEN KISS

Riding next to you

With Springsteen on the stereo

Is just perfect

As we drive the endless miles

Through the rolling green mountains

Sprinkled with last night's snow

I adore the way your eyes sparkle

When I regale you with the stories

And memories from long ago

Your face... freckled with smiles

Sweet sounds of laughter

Fill the car

Outside the shiny glow of melted snow

Forms puddles all along the street

The red traffic light's reflection beams brightly

A feast for these thirsty eyes

As I lean in

To steal a kiss...before the light turns green....

CAROUSEL

A million thoughts

Crashing … colliding inside

Imprisoned on this carousel of recurrence

Waiting for the song to stop

Waiting for my feet to touch the ground

So I can catch up to you again

JILL AND TOBY

It was just like a dream

Holding you tightly

While the magic in the air

Turned to gold

Your whispers were soft and delicate

The nearly invisible words

Arrived gently

From impassioned breath

And even now when I look down

At the band of gold on my ring finger

I can still feel your skin on my hands

Because you melt right through me

No matter how many years pass

You will remain the one I always dreamed of

The one I was supposed to meet

The light that cannot be dimmed

POSSIBILITIES

We talk in possibilities

And see in dreams

Of shadowed moonlit rains

We sense in creations

And dream in sights

Of timed perforations

We search in patterns

And take in hoards

Of half-forgotten longings

We feel in riddles

And give in steps

Of tensioned ecstasies

REMEMBERING SUMMER ON A JANUARY DAY

Red and green

Christmas lights

Circle my windows inside

And silvery icicle lights

Surround the back porch door

Signaling winter

But as I sit on my back porch today

In my green Adirondack chair

With my iPod on shuffle

I am in short sleeves

And my bare arms are warmed

By a sunbaked breeze

When the Indigo Girls sing, "Mystery"

It immediately carries me back

To a summer

When we were in love

And the image of us

In a secluded spot

On a tan blanket

Beside the banks of the Folly river

Plays like a movie inside my head

We used to lie on our backs

And count the clouds

While watching giant dragonflies

Hover

Over the sparkling wetlands

Lying on that blanket

Holding your hand

I never felt closer to you

We rarely spoke a word

Choosing to embrace the beauty of silence instead

A flock of big Hitchcock looking black birds

Squawk overhead

Ushering in a dark cloud

That mocks my reflections

Dimming this fair January sky

IMPOSSIBILITY

A flash that begins with the eyes

Dances between two hearts

Matching desires

Intersect

Between two

Living separate lives

Laughter echoes

Inside impossible dreams

Like a memory in waiting

Too stubborn to ever fade away

SURROUNDED BY YOUR STORM

I fall into your darkness

And there is no other place

I would rather be

Than surrounded by your storm

JASON'S BEACH HOUSE

We are here in Cape May at Jason's summer beach house. It's a weather-bleached cottage of sorts, perfectly located just blocks from the beach with a large front porch and a deck out back. The weather has finally cooperated in New Jersey, so Ricardo, Valentino, and I are here for the weekend. Valentino, by the way, is Ricardo's yellow Labrador. His name suits him well, since he greets everyone warmly, especially the female Labs, but that is a story for another time.

Sitting on the beach, in my deluxe beach chair with the drink holders, I write this piece, feeling relaxed and calm. Ricardo has joined in a beach volleyball game and the bikini-clad girls are already vying for his attention. I laugh out loud when I see this. If they only knew!

Jason is already several minutes into his late morning nap. The consummate surfer, Jason was up at 5am to catch high tide waves. He always naps right before lunchtime. Maria, Jason's girlfriend, sits across from me deeply engrossed in the book she is reading. I catch her every now and again observing Jason asleep. I like that she notices him. Her eyes are never far from him, and he deserves to have someone who looks at him like that.

She and I have bonded already on this trip when the two of us scoped out the newly arrived paperbacks over at the second hand bookstore. We share a passion for words and books, and each one of us came away with an armful yesterday. She is interesting and genuine. Two things Jason's ex never was.

The water has been glorious. At least once an hour the four of us make a return visit. I love watching the kids with their boogie boards riding in the waves with gigantic grins on their faces. Seeing them reminds me of how I was at their age. I only came out of the water for lunch and hated waiting the standard 30 minutes afterwards before a return trip to the water was allowed.

So far I have made blueberry pancakes and French toast for breakfast. I love cooking breakfast; it's a summer ritual now. Jason wakes me up in the morning when he returns from surfing and he keeps me company in the open air kitchen until it is time to rouse the others from their sleep.

Our weekend progresses nicely with our lazy beach days. In the evenings, we take long walks on quiet out of the way roads and admire the old beach houses. I love the sounds of evenings at the Cape May shoreline. Voices echo and the ocean is always heard as the backbeat.

We read until our eyes are heavy, swapping books among ourselves. I am most affected by "The Complete Stories and Poems of Lewis Carroll", and recommend it without reservation to anyone who has ever loved a storyteller or a poet.

We feast on hamburgers and hot dogs and we ride our bikes over to the boardwalk to search out the artists, hoping their creativity will rub off on us. We visit a kite maker, where for a few moments, I think about Michael, and remember the first kite I ever bought him. It was in the shape of Batman and I can still see that black kite hovering high above the dunes. Michael is 21 now, too old to be given a kite for a graduation gift I suppose.

Jason makes his famous rum and ginger beer drinks as we settle down for a game of scrabble on the front porch. Afterwards we walk down to the boardwalk for fresh peach ice cream, the prize for the winning scrabble game team.

At the end of the weekend, we are finally unwound, rested, and making our way back up north. In the car, we snack on salt water taffy while the music from my iPod thankfully drowns out the sound of Valentino snoring in the back seat!

REFLECTIONS

Looking glass reflections

Illustrate a night graced with intimate stillness

An irrepressible peace

Trickles effortlessly through our fingers

And later… into dreams

BROKEN

For a while the magic took

But soon the cracks began to seep through

To the other side of love's dream

And now

Broken

Is a lonely place to be

Nothing fits

Scattered pieces

Beg to be reunited

Outside

The raindrops fall heavily on concrete sidewalks

Puddles form reflective pools of pain

That he steps over and around

Afraid of feeling

Afraid of remembering

Afraid of seeing himself

In the watery mirror

It is much easier

To walk past

With eyes focused straight ahead

Pretending to be busy

Pretending to be ambitious

Pretending to have it all together

When the truth is …

Deep inside …

He is broken …

A HEART'S REPRIEVE

The white winged dove

Landed in my heart

When faith had all but ceased

<u>\<SIGH\></u>

Standing together against time

The humming of the ocean

Your hand in mine

Completely lost in the moment

When everything feels right

...\<sigh\>.....

A WORK OF ART

When there is true love

All we need is a soul

Without eyes to see

To make our lives

Into a work of art

EVEN IN COFFEE SHOPS

Sitting in Starbucks

Some guy taps my shoulder

Starts talking

It's been a while

I can't speak

And yet it feels all

Kind of familiar

Like that day

On the floor

Of Alicia's living room

It was the fourth of July

And you

The handsome stranger

Sat beside me

Is this possible?

Probably not

So I figure

That's why

This guy

Wants to share his scone at my table

Because some people just know things

And some know when others don't

As I suppose is the case here

So I return his smile

And don't recoil his touch

Because I know

There are signs

Even in coffee shops

<u>RECOVERING HOPE</u>

At dusk

The emptiness sways back and forth

Like the recently vacant swing

In the park across the street

When night begins to fall upon the surface

He stares up at the naked sky

Trying to recover the hope

He once so clearly imagined

RESOLUTE

The word that is bouncing around my head today as I try to write is "resolute." I don't know why I have chosen that word to capture what I feel right now. It just seems right.

And once again I have no idea what I will write. It just comes ... like a stream. However, today it is not gushing out. It is more a slow meandering trickle. I feel the pauses between words and my breath.

Remember when you were a kid out in the woods? You could have city streets infringing on all sides but once you were in the woods you felt a world apart. As a child growing up in Westfield, my entire backyard was woods and trees. After a sleepover, my friends and I would get up and go outside to the woods. We would go in all sorts of weather. It didn't matter. Back then, as kids, we were challenged to get creative for our entertainment. And we did! Our imaginations took us off to faraway places with magic swords, knights, and dragons. Whatever the game, we all believed. The woods behind my house extended so far that you could hear a pin drop, making it easy for us to transport ourselves into another place and time.

In winter we would all pile into the toboggan for a wild ride down the snow covered hill. We would scream in excitement until we landed safely at the bottom. When

we were older we would take a ride only after we had been around the neighborhood shoveling driveways and sidewalks for money.

I loved that backyard and how the sun would filter through the trees so early in the morning...and that gentle kind of sunlight ... light golden ... which created leafy shadows that would envelope us as we stepped outside. It really didn't matter what we were doing or what we ended up with ... it was the whole process of sharing the experience with your friends which mattered most. We were creating a memory.

My old house and its woods are no longer there. A few years after my parents sold the house it was bulldozed in favor of newly constructed houses and a street, but now when I look at pictures of the old house on Rahway Avenue ... it all comes rushing back ... as if nothing ever changed.

FOR ROB AND STACY

Standing here before friends and family

She appears

The love of his life

Bouquet in hand

She glows in white

One tear streams slowly down his face

As the bonds of forever are now in place

UNDER THE SHELTER OF YOUR OLD TURNTABLE

As evening slips away

We wrap ourselves

In the warm embrace

Of each other's arms

Under the shelter

Of your old turntable

Listening to the vinyl records

Of Fleetwood Mac

And for a moment

We are back to being teenagers

Falling in love

With the last trace

Of "The Chain" on our mouths

" I can still hear you saying you would never break the chain."

AGAINST A RISING AUGUST MOON

Late summer lethargy

Naps on my chest

A delicate heaviness

That holds everything at bay

And as the languid evening

Eases into darkness

We follow the flight

Of the night birds

Lazily sipping our pink lemonade

Predicting an Indian summer

When our eyes grow heavy

The wind finds its voice

Whispering promises

While cooling

Our sun-kissed skin

As we dance to the dulcet sounds

Of Stevie Nicks

Against a rising August moon

THE DAY YOUR SORROW BECAME MINE

Afternoon gray drips gradually from the sky

Splashing shade

All across these streets

Secret pain lies awake

Within the shadows

Of the midday heat

And when you pass by

With your eyes down

Your sorrow becomes mine

UNSEEN BEAUTY

He doesn't see the beauty

Countless others can see

He doesn't feel the warmth

So calming to the touch

He doesn't hear the magnificence

Resounding all around

For just one day

I wish

I could lend him my eyes

So when he looks in the mirror, he'd only see love staring back

I guess every one of us

Is a little bit broken inside

FILLING EACH OTHER'S ACHING VOID

Sprawled across my bed

We fill each other's aching void

Listening to the wind swirl and spin

Up against the frost covered window

It is so easy to imagine being in love

Snuggled under the covers

Watching the snow

Catch the last rays of lingering sunlight

And as I watch you sleep

I know how contentment feels

In this wintry afternoon

With your hand entwined in mine

THE SOUND OF YOUR VOICE

A single word

Spoken by you

And the sound of your voice

Is enough to draw my attention

To raise my head from my self-absorbed introspection

To notice that I am not alone today

Or ever

<u>SO UNDENIABLY US</u>

Our exposed edges

Pierce

Our floating

Iridescence

So with kid-gloves

And some spit and polish

We piece together

The puzzle

That is so undeniably us

FINGERPRINTS ON HIS HEART

Wild and wind- tossed

She blew through his life

Like a torrential downpour

Temperature so hot

She melted

Even the rain

Edgy and untamed

She was a fistful of sand

He could not hold

She left him ... her bridegroom

Empty and alone

With her fingerprints on his heart

SKY OF DREAMS

Put your head on my chest

And lie with me

Beneath the sky of dreams

Where time is forever frozen

And the world stands still

POSTSCRIPT

What do you write when no one is looking?

I've been thinking about what makes for "good" writing and I think part of it is the writer's ability to let down the walls and the defenses and just be real and tangible. Good writing arises from true self. There is no pretense or affectation. It just is. You believe it and feel it from deep inside. Good writing is an awakening. We begin to remember things we haven't felt in years. As we read there is this pivotal moment where you want to yell out, "Yes, I have seen this, felt this, and lived this!" There is a validation of the truth, connecting all of us to each other and to the human condition.

In my opinion, the best writing comes when nobody is looking.

Good writing seldom cries out, "*Look at me, look at me!*" It isn't based upon intellect, social status, or even education. The people who believe that the quality of a piece of writing is based upon these exterior parameters are only fooling themselves. Techniques and mechanics do not

make a writer. These things can be learned, but they alone are not the substance of good writing.

It is my belief that there is no substitute for the heart and soul of a writer. The writing happens when there is no applause and it happens despite ridicule and torment. Writing prevails through tragedy and circumstance. It does not arise from the receipt of a token or praise. A writer does not need the external world to validate their passion. It just is. It is like breathing. It is a must have. The words come of their own volition regardless and in spite of the world. And when a reader relates to the writer's words, that is the icing on the cake, so to speak.

So back to my original question, "*What do you write when nobody is looking?*" This is probably going to be your best writing. Don't fear it or yourself. Just let the words spill onto the page.

Robert A. Cozzi

Made in the USA
Middletown, DE
09 July 2021